RESISTANCE TRAINING FOR ICE HOCKEY

CHRIS LUTZ

Copyright © 2016 Lutz

All rights reserved.

ISBN-13: 978-1537441078

ISBN-10: 1537441078

DEDICATION

I dedicate this book to all the hard working young players out there.

CONTENTS

INTRODUCTION 1

RESISTANCE TRAINING PRINCIPLES TO FOLLOW 12

BASIC MUSCULAR ANATOMY 14

RESISTANCE TRAINING FOR HOCKEY ROUTINES 43

COACHING AND ON ICE PRACTICE SPECIFICS 55

PRACTICE STRATEGY 57

EXERCISE PICTURE DEMONSTRATIONS 63

LOWER BODY EXERCISES 63

CHEST SHOULDER AND TRICEP EXERCISES 70

UPPER BACK, REAR SHOULDER, BICEP EXERCISES 84

ABDOMINAL, LOWER BACK, AND NECK EXERCISES 93

RESISTANCE TRAINING FOR HOCKEY PROGRESS CHART .. 102

ABOUT THE AUTHOR 103

Lutz

ACKNOWLEDGMENTS

I'd like to acknowledge all of the prior coaches who came before me and contributed to helping me learn what I know today.

INTRODUCTION

Hockey is a popular sport and getting more popular every year. I played at the highest levels I could in Virginia and Maryland growing up as a kid. At the time, Maryland schools had an interscholastic league, but none of the Virginia schools had teams. Within the last 20 years every school now has a team. Hockey's popularity is continuing to expand ever more into those southern territories to where it is quite popular in many parts of Florida.

Hockey is also a high force and high volume activity. It can be brutal and exhausting for players. There is an entire industry built around improving hockey skills and your game in general.

As far as fitness for hockey goes, the issue is probably mostly centered around two points.

1. Injury prevention.
2. Increased strength and power development for performance.

What might be more valuable in programming like this is what you DON'T want to do. As far as the skill conditioning of hockey is concerned, that is something that is specific to each skill. Motor skills are very specific, meaning, exact in nature.

The old saying perfect practice makes perfect applies here. All of the various tools, devices, and programs that are imitating a hockey skill, in an attempt to improve the user's skill, are probably producing the opposite. There are a few types of skill transfer you need to be concerned with.

1. Positive transfer-Practicing with your stick and all the same equipment and a non-weighted puck will produce a positive transfer to the game.

2. Negative transfer-Practicing your stickhandling with a weighted puck or some other device that is not your exact piece of equipment you'll use in the game, will result in a negative transfer, or a worsening of your skill.

3. Neutral transfer-Training your body in preparation for the sport, according to muscle and joint function, will result in a neutral transfer, meaning, that you are stronger and fitter, but there is no adverse effects on your skills.

That's what we want. To improve your strength, power, and injury resistance so that you can take that to practice and apply it to refine your skills specifically. We will not try to combine skill practice and conditioning for the sport together. That's a sport science mistake that has been going on for decades.

This is confirmed for us.
"Luttgens and Hamilton (1997), in their book on kinesiology about the specificity of neuromuscular patterns: "Skillful and efficient performance in a particular technique can be developed only by practice of that technique. Only in this way can the necessary adjustments in the neuromuscular

mechanism be made to ensure a well-coordinated movement. (p. 507)."

"Strength or endurance training activities must be specific to the demands of the particular activity for which strength or endurance is being developed. The full range of joint action, the speed, and the resistance demands of the movement pattern should be duplicated in the training activity (p. 465)."

Too often coaches and athletes get caught up in dogma and tradition that has been passed down without any real substance. It's that last portion of the second quote above that is important and forgotten in sport training. The resistance demands of the movement pattern should be duplicated. If you're generally trying to develop strength and power, you will need to employ greater overloading resistances. That's for strength and power.

But, for skill training. Fine motor skills, need to be finely tuned and repetitively practiced perfectly. For example, the weighted puck, again, is not the same resistance demands for a fine motor skill like stickhandling. It's not the same for a powerful gross motor skill like shooting that requires accuracy.

You might think, "Well, if I can handle a heavier puck, I'll naturally be good at a lighter puck." That might seem intuitive at first. We see that with batters in baseball warming up with a weight on their bat.

Here's another example from a different sport.

Imagine shooting three pointers in basketball, but instead you used a three pound medicine ball. Something significantly heavier than a game ball.

You'd need to dial in enough power to get it to the hoop with enough accuracy to make it in. It may take you 10 tries to even dial in the distance. What you're doing is training your nervous system to gauge the output you need to accomplish that.

Ok, so you've practiced and developed a little skill. Now, it's game time. Immediately go back to that game ball you'll be playing with. What do you think will happen on the first shot you take? You'll fire it over the hoop, right? Why? Because your motor skills were practiced and dialed in for a skill with different resistance demands. And it will probably take you at least 10 more tries to get back used to the game ball again. This is a negative skill transfer and the worst thing you could do besides injure yourself when you're trying to improve your game.

The same thing can apply in any sport. It just may be less noticeable in a more linear game like hockey.

The same can hold true for conditioning your body on a chemical level, not just with motor skills and muscular output. I'll use another personal example to demonstrate the principle.

One year, I had dedicated my summer to football conditioning which consisted mostly of general weight training and sprint type conditioning. By the time fall came around and it was time to try out for hockey, I was excited because I knew I was already in good "shape." And I was. I was fit and strong. However, that kind of conditioning had no transfer whatsoever to my hockey conditioning. It was as if I hadn't trained at all and I was so exhausted, I performed very poorly and made a B team when I should have been on an A team that year. It was all due to a poor try out. Of course, after a week or two of hockey, I was right back where I was before.

Running sprints had no transfer at all to my hockey skating conditioning. It wasn't good and it wasn't bad. It was just neutral. Like I never did anything. My skating condition could have deteriorated, because I was neglecting it, while my running condition improved. It's a strange feeling, but this is how the body works.

Conversely, the following year, I was more into hockey. I played for a good coach during the season and chose to take his summer ice coaching sessions that summer. He was known for his emphasis on skating conditioning for players. He also knew of my aspirations to play for a higher level team that fall. He pushed me hard all summer. That fall I went back to school and, when tested, ran the best mile run time I'd ever had with ease. However, I had not run once during the summer.

Interestingly, in this instance skating conditioning had a positive conditioning transfer to running performance. But, prior to that, running conditioning had no transfer to skating conditioning.

For the purposes of this book, we'll be separating

general strength and power development and hockey skill specific practice. Towards the end of this book, there will be recommendations for how to organize training and practice such that you can maximize both depending on the phase of the season in which you are currently playing.

WHY CORE AND FUNCTIONAL TRAINING IS INFERIOR

First and foremost, let's define "core" training. Well, we can't because a definition doesn't exist. Therein lies the problem. That is why the word core is set off in quotes. It is nothing more than a buzz word in the industry right now. It has no meaning and every trainer and therapist out there claims it is every person's weakest area and they know how to fix it. Somehow the advancements in technology, knowledge and machinery have taken a back seat to retrospective, backward, primitive thinking in that this can all be fixed with a simple rubber ball. This backward thinking appears to be in line with the current bashing of modern Western medicine and science in general by the layperson. If science has no meaning no knowledge can be attained and you can do whatever you please in total chaos. The phrase "core training" is also used synonymously with the phrase "functional training" which does not have a definition either. Either you or a part of you functions or you/it doesn't. This section is designed to educate you about abdominal structure and function as well as to expose the fallacy of the ideas of "core" and "functional" training particularly in relation to training for hockey.

Here is what the problem is. "Core" conditioning advocates believe that machines do not engage the stabilizing muscles presumably in the abdomen and lower back. That's false. Many muscles in your body can act as stabilizers or even neutralizers, which is a different concept altogether, but most don't know what it is so it is never mentioned.

When you use the tricep extension machine, you almost can't breathe because your abdominal wall is so contracted to stabilize your trunk to push down on a heavy load. That's a high degree of stabilization in action.

Second, muscles develop better when worked directly. Why would you do an exercise for your biceps in the hopes of improving your abdominals? You wouldn't do a calf raise to neurologically coordinate with your triceps would you? A simple and straight forward abdominal exercise would be more effective.

Worse yet still, is that many exercises believed to be for the abdominals are not actually abdominal exercises at all or only in a stabilizing manner. Muscles develop best being used dynamically or actually moving against resistance as opposed to a non-moving static or stabilizing contraction only. Usually it is the hip flexor group that people mistake for abdominal work and the abdominals are just stabilizing in this instance. Anything you see on TV for abdominal exercise is really for the hip flexor group. You are not working the abdominals unless the spine is flexing or bending forward. Anything that causes the hip joint to move, is hip flexor muscle activity. If you lie on the ground on your back and raise and lower straight legs, a common and contraindicated exercise, you are flexing the hip.

It is contraindicated meaning we, as professionals, do not prescribe it to clients because of its high probability of injury. Specifically back injury. The vertebrae slip forward and can even break at the pars interarticularis or the facet joints. This has been documented well with X-ray studies. This is because the hip flexor region originates from the sides of the lumbar vertebrae and runs diagonally through the body and inserts on the top portion of the femur or thigh bone. Obviously when it shortens it moves (flexes) the hip. The abdominals play no part in that other than stabilization.

Fig. 1 is a good simple diagram to help you unravel the mountain of mysteries contained in your abdominal wall. A. is the Linea Alba-this is just a line of connective tissue not a division of 2 muscles. B. is the Rectus Abdominus-the main abdominal muscle. It flexes the lumbar spine and compresses the abdomen to aid in forced expiration. NOTE: The rectus abdominus is ONE muscle it is not 6 or 8 little ones. *There is no such thing as the upper and lower abdominals.* C. is the External Oblique-it flexes the spine to the front, laterally, and rotates the spine and compresses the abdomen. D. is the Internal Oblique-it flexes the spine, compresses abdomen, and rotates spine. E. is the Transversus Abdominus-it's one and only function is to compress the abdomen for forced expiration, urination, defecation and child birth. F. is the Rectus Sheath-another layer of connective tissue. If done correctly, most abdominal exercises that flex the spine addresses all of these functions of the entire abdominal wall. A simple crunch on the floor with soles of the feet flat together and knees out to the side do a pretty good job for a beginner. You can make it progressive by adding weight plates for resistance. However, there is no stretching in a floor crunch.

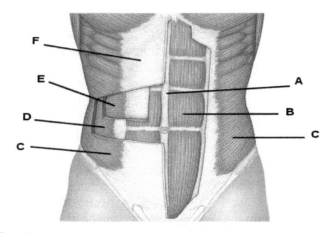

Fig. 1
The transversus abdominus is probably the least understood muscle of the entire abdominal wall. If you talk to any other trainer/therapist from any other organization you will probably tell you that it is the weakest muscle in your body and is the cause of many postural and neurological problems. They will then proceed to prescribe an arbitrary and lengthy program of stability ball, medicine ball, and rubber tubing exercises to "fix" or "correct" it. However, I just listed its function for you and very few of those exercises are going to be helpful for it. How could they be? Those exercises don't address its function. You would get more activity for that muscle by coughing or sneezing very hard rather than performing any of those exercises. This represents a clear lack of understanding of anatomy and kinesiology. If someone is trying to prescribe an exercise routine for you for hockey fitness with this premise, you can be sure it's incorrect.

A majority of the fitness industry has moved in this

direction. Many professional athletes are trained in this manner too not knowing that their training routine actually *violates* motor learning and skill principles as opposed to enhancing skill. Nothing can be done in a gym to enhance skill on a field. Skill can only be enhanced by practicing that skill exactly. That includes similar, but not exact activities where if the resistance demands are different, it is a different skill altogether. Develop strength generally and practice skills specifically or identically. That is the most efficient means to improve an athlete's condition and performance.

Many people have a hard time controlling and utilizing their abdominals. I believe most of this stems partly from poor motor control and mostly from lack of knowledge about the structure and function of the abdominal structures. They are really very simple in function and that is why I included the diagram above.

RESISTANCE TRAINING PRINCIPLES TO FOLLOW

Now that we've established all of the above and gotten it out of the way, let's get down to what you should be doing. We will be specifically focusing and emphasizing the muscles used while playing hockey. In that sense, it will be "sport specific". However, the exercises you'll be performing won't look like hockey. We need to train those bodily structures according to their muscle and joint functions, not according to the skill or activity. So, for example, there is a high degree trunk rotation in hockey. We will be focusing on the mid-section musculature like the obliques and lumbar rotators. We will naturally include lower back extension and rotary torso exercises, but they will not resemble the hockey swing.

Included with your program you'll find 8 weeks of varied routines for hockey training. Each workout routine will be continued for 2 weeks each to allow for learning and progression.

When deciding on exercise to engage in, it is important that we recognize activities that are **safe, effective, and efficient and in that order**. Here are a few basic definitions for the beginners.

A _repetition_ is one single lifting and lowering motion of a resistance in any given exercise. It could also be a singular application of effort such as in the case of a static technique or a negative only rep which is just the lowering phase. A _set_ is a group of repetitions performed together. The *positive* is the lifting of the resistance. The *negative* is the lowing of the resistance regardless of what the bar or body is doing. Performing repetitions in a slow, controlled, fluid movement is of the utmost importance.

The most important part of each repetition is the changes in direction at the top and bottom of each movement. That is where there is likely to be too much acceleration or jerky sudden movements or starts and stops. You want none of those. Some exercises will require a pause and/or a squeeze technique at the top of the movement; others will require a smooth and perpetual motion transfer from the positive directly into the negative.

And there are different modes of exercise meaning the kind of exercise or the tool used. For example, a barbell bench press, the dumbbell bench press, and machine chest press are the same exercise using 3 different modes.

Many people may hinder their own progress by not looking at exercise in the proper context. They may get too hung up on actually trying to move the resistance when in actuality the whole point is to get to a point where it is impossible to move (to reach muscular fatigue) to stimulate desired changes. This is the *overload principle*. You must subject the body to regular stresses that it is not accustomed to. Hence, the term overload.

BASIC MUSCULAR ANATOMY

A. Pectoralis major
B. Anterior deltoid
C. Sternocleidomastoid
D. Obliques
E. Rectus abdominus
F. Biceps brachii
G. Triceps brachii
H. Wrist flexor group
I. Wrist extensor group
J. Serratus anterior
K. Hip flexor group (Iliopsoas)
L. Lastissimus dorsi
M. Posterior deltoid
N. Trapezius (I-IV)
O. Erector spinae
P. Quadriceps
Q. Hamstrings
R. Gastrocnemius/soleus
S. Adductors
T. Gluteus maxiums
U. Tensor fascia latae/Iliotibial band
V. Tibialis Anterior

The below diagram is in anatomical neutral position which all directional terms are referenced from. Below are the major muscle groups listed and their primary actions at the joints. This is NOT all of the actions. For example, the triceps brachii crosses the elbow and the shoulder and contributes to extending the shoulder in addition to flexing the elbow. Many muscles can have many functions and cross more than one joint. For our purposes here, we will focus on the major muscle groups' primary actions.

Major Muscle	Primary Action
Pectoralis Major	Horizontally adducts humerus bone
Anterior Deltoid	Horizontally adducts humerus bone at shoulder and adducts humerus
Sternocleidomastoid	Rotates and flexes the neck
Obliques	Rotates and laterally flexes the spine
Rectus Abdominus	Flexes the lumbar spine
Biceps Brachii	Supinates the hand and flexes the elbow
Triceps Brachii	Extends the elbow
Wrist Flexor group	Flexes the wrist and fingers
Wrist Extensor group	Extends the wrist and fingers
Serratus Anterior	Protracts the shoulder girdle
Hip Flexor (Iliopsoas)	Flexes the hip
Latissimus Dorsi	Extends the shoulder and horizontally abducts the shoulder
Posterior Deltoid	Extends and horizontally abducts the shoulder
Trapezius (I-IV)	Retracts and elevates the scapula

Erector Spinae	Extends the lumbar spine
Quadriceps	Extends the knee
Hamstrings	Flexes the knee and extends hip
Gastrocnemius/soleus	Plantar flexes the ankle (bent and straight knee)
Adductor group	Adducts the hip
Gluteus Maximus	Abducts and extends the hip
Tensor Fascia Latae	Abducts the hip
Tibialis Anterior	Dorsi flexes the ankle

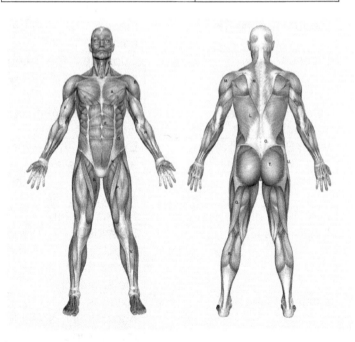

Stretching and Warm-up

Why isn't there any formal warm-up, stretching or cool-down? Contrary to popular belief, your muscles will perform better if they are slightly cooler. Heat contributes to fatigue and ultimately heat sickness. We actually want to keep you cool during a workout. Frequently, a warm up is more dangerous than the exercise itself because of the high forces involved which you'll read more about shortly. Your first two or three sub maximal repetitions are the warm up. It only takes a few seconds to bring your body temperature up. If you feel like you need a warm up set, go ahead and informally do a submaximal one, but only to prepare, try not to dip into any reserves you might have for your real working set effort.

Usually walking around for a couple minutes after a workout is sufficient to prevent any negative post exercise effects.

Stretching does not offer any protection from injury as previously thought. Generally, we prescribe full range of motion exercises which includes emphasizing the stretching portion of the range. This is one way, but not the only way you can enhance flexibility through strength training.

Exercise selection

Generally speaking, resistance training is performed in a circuit of succeeding exercises. You can use a mixture of machines, free weights, cables, body weight, and manual resistance depending on program design. The more linear or compound movements can all be done with free weights, but rotary movements are sometimes best accomplished with the use of machines depending on manufacturer. Anywhere from 6-15 exercises, generally speaking, may be used to work the whole body utilizing all the major muscle groups. You should almost always arrange the exercises in a push/pull fashion so as to work opposing muscle groups continuously without too much rest between exercises. And we usually start with the biggest muscle groups first and work down to smaller muscle groups to finish the routine such as neck, calf, and forearm exercises.

Frequency

Two to three days per week is the standard for resistance training. Start with 3, but realize over time that you may need more rest days here or there to fully recover and maximize potential. This will vary from person to person. A good starting schedule would be 3 whole body workouts performed on Monday, Wednesday, and Friday. Then your body gets 2 full recovery days and you start over again.

Sets

Resistance training typically utilizes one set ending in a 100% effort to muscular fatigue. Some trainees will use as many as three, but these are usually in the form of a warm up set or advanced overload techniques such as a breakdown or post fatigue negatives. I almost always need a warm up set for the barbell squat and bench press, myself. Usually a few reps of the movement with just the bar will do.   We'll go into more on advanced techniques later.

Rest

Ideally, try to move as quickly as possible to the next exercise to maintain the elevated heart rate for cardiovascular conditioning as well as muscular work.   Shoot for no longer than 30 seconds between exercises. That should allow ample time to go to the next exercise, set it, get strapped in, and start.   Rest between workouts should be exactly that. Recovery days are not meant to be filled in with more intense or long duration activity in the hopes of improving or "burning" more. Because of the fact that we are combining muscular and cardiovascular work on the same days, that leaves a maximum amount of recovery time and, therefore, more progress, not less. Adequate rest is critically important to continued progress. All the positive adaptations occur then. You don't want to, and must not interrupt the process.   The goal should be to keep your stresses as close together as possible and maximize your rest time, don't fill it in.   Generally, everyone should do well on the frequency laid out above.

Resistance

Resistance should be about 80% of 1 repetition maximum (1RM). I'm not a proponent of frequent "maxing out" because of the safety issues involved especially for adolescents and elderly, but you can quickly, over the course of a few workouts, find the weight that causes you to fatigue in the prescribed number of repetitions. Higher repetition ranges can be used for adolescents or possibly the elderly in the 12-20 rep range, obviously using a lower percentage of 1 rep max. Again, to be more accurate without subjecting yourself to danger, use the following formula to establish a close estimate of your "max".

Predicted 1RM= Weight Lifted / (1.0278 - .0278X) where X = the number of reps performed.

Take 70-80% of your one rep max to get a good training weight to start and progress from there.

Repetitions

This is a little trickier. It could all depend on how much you want to gain in strength or endurance and also upon what repetition speed or cadence you use. Resistance training authorities traditionally espouse a two second lifting phase and a four second lowering phase. A one second pause and squeeze technique is inserted if it is a single joint movement (bicep curl). No pause if it's a multi joint pushing movement (leg press) NOTE: This is probably the fastest you could ever move safely during exercise. Using that speed, you could do as many as eight-12 repetitions in about one minute or a little over. Using something slower like a 10/10 cadence would result in as little as two repetitions and maybe a maximum of eight. A one minute chin exercise could be one rep (30 seconds up, 30 seconds down). It will all depend on your rep cadence.

Time Under Load

You could also use Time Under Load (TUL) as your guide. We have found a range of 40-70 seconds to be about right for muscular strength and endurance improvements regardless of rep speed. Instead of or in addition to counting reps, you can use a stop watch to document set duration. Minutes and seconds may be a little more accurate than counting whole reps. You can analyze it two ways. If you are counting reps and are trying to get to 12 to progress the resistance, but always end up at 11 and have used other techniques to try to progress beyond that level, but can't seem to then this is where TUL will be useful. You may perform 11 reps, but the next time you workout might be 20 more seconds or so. This is progress that you would not have otherwise seen unless you were timing your set. You can try to perform a little more time each workout on any given exercise as another method of progress. More intriguing is if you see consistent TUL's over a few workouts, this could mean that your body and those specific muscles have a specific rate at which you fatigue almost no matter what. If your reps and time are consistent with good form, try a small resistance increase. If it is still consistent, try another small resistance increase the next workout. Here I am describing single progression using only resistance and keeping reps and/or time consistent. It should happen on its own without manipulation by you.

Progression

This is a biggie. Almost no trainees I've seen document their progress. I highly recommend using a progress chart (provided) to show improvements in resistance and reps or time. Use triple progression. Always try to perform 1 more rep, a little more time, or use slightly more resistance than last time in good form. It is unlikely that two or more of these will increase from workout to workout. It is likely that you will improve on one measure or another once past the initial beginner workouts. It is NOT purposely increasing two or more measures from workout to workout. That will not last long at all in terms of progress and remember, our upper rep limit is likely to be around 12 so that can't increase every workout. Just strive to improve one of the three from workout to workout.

Variety is important because the body is an adaptable organism. This approach reasonably varies your routine constantly to continue progress without doing a different routine every time and rendering your records kept useless. Keep in mind that the major determining factor for progression in *resistance training* is resistance levels so if your TUL's come out to be relatively consistent, continue to progress in resistance in small increments. Over time this adds up to be huge gains. Over a little longer time frame, vary your routines. Try not to stagnate or retrogress.

Duration

For advanced trainees, workouts could be as little as 15 or as long as 45 minutes, but generally a workout lasts 20-30 minutes. For those with orthopedic injuries, the workout may end up being a little longer. 45 minutes should be the maximum time any person should be doing *continuous* activity and still hope to improve. Some guy's workouts last in the hours, but I am talking about actual exercise time. If your workout takes one hour plus, but you're sitting and relaxing or talking for the majority of it, I'd venture to guess that actual working time is still around the 20-30 minute mark. I have finished whole body workouts in the time it takes some people to finish 3 sets of an. That is a dramatic demonstration of how inefficient most training plans are and how much gym time is wasted.

Alignment and Positioning

Compound exercises: Get as reasonably close to the bar as possible (to allow comfortable stretching) if it is a pushing exercise and get as far away as is reasonably possible (to allow stretching) if it is a pulling exercise. Record the settings. This is positioning. You will also want to consider planar alignment with the your limbs on a compound exercise. For example, on an upright chest press machine, you do not want the seat too low or too high to where the relative linear path of your arms are not in line with the path of the machine's movement arm on the same plane.

Simple exercises: Line up the axis of your joint that will be moving with the axis of the machine. Record the settings. This is alignment. Note: Some exercises are actually multi-joint, but operate like a simple exercise. An example is some abdominal and lower back machines. Every space between vertebrae is a joint, but in this case, use alignment principles with the machine's singular axis of rotation.

Advanced Resistance Training for Hockey

Over the course of time, you may need to prescribe some advanced techniques to help you continue to make good progress or vary the routine. The techniques most commonly used by resistance training trainees are below. Many of these have plenty of evidence of effectiveness behind them. Some others are more rooted in philosophy of what should work exceptionally well, they just may not have been tested thoroughly yet. And some are just different ways of performing exercise, but still under the same umbrella of principles. Let's take a look.

Post fatigue negatives

At the end of a normal set of reps to fatigue, your positive strength has been exhausted, but you are always about 40-60% stronger on the negative contraction than the positive. This is an opportunity to inroad a little further. In this example, you need a partner that will lift the resistance for you to perform a few more negative contractions slowly lowering the resistance until the last one you almost cannot stop the descent. Usually three or so will do the trick.

Slow Training

Standard rep speed is a cadence of 2/4. Slower speeds or cadences make the exercise harder for your muscles to lift the same resistance adding a new stimulus possibly in spite of lower resistance levels. These can be cadences of 5/5, 10/10, as long as 30 seconds to 1 minute or any combination thereof. An example would be the performance of a 1 minute chin. You take 30 seconds to lift your body in the chin up and 30 seconds to come down. The same can be done for dips or any other exercise if equipment allows. Challenging to say the least even with just body weight!

Breakdowns

Breakdown training is another form of advanced training to stimulate further progress. It consists of using the your regular training weight in a set to fatigue and then immediately reduce the resistance 20-30% and do a few more reps to fatigue. This can be done once or as many times as you choose. This is noted on the progress chart as a downward staircase.

Forced Reps

Forced reps is a technique used where your partner will assist on the lifting phase of several more reps after you have fatigued on your own. The partner does not help on the negative portion of the assisted reps. The partner should provide enough force for the trainee to just barely continue movement despite a maximal effort to finish one or two more reps. If done correctly, the trainee should not feel the partner helping on the positive phase. It will be a slow process finishing that last rep as the partner is providing only enough to overcome the rate of fatigue of the trainee's muscles. It may take 10 seconds or more in some cases. 1 forced rep is intense and more up to 3 can be extremely taxing.

Pre-exhaustion/Post-exhaustion

Pre-exhaustion is one of the most used forms of advanced training. It is really an attempt to circumvent a weak link in a chain. Imagine doing a set of machine chest flies immediately followed by the chest press. What happened? You pre-exhausted the larger musculature (pecorals or chest) with the first exercise and followed it with a compound exercise that also uses the triceps which are still fresh to more thoroughly work the chest. In the bench press alone, the triceps are the weak link because they are smaller and this is a way around that. This principle can be applied to any group of muscles and even applied in reverse which is post-exhaustion.

Negative Only

Negative only has been promoted as the best technique so far developed. Since you are about 40-60% stronger on any given negative movement, this technique, as the name implies, uses only the negative portion of the rep. The chin up is an excellent exercise to use for this technique. Start by getting into the top position by standing on something and ease into the transfer of weight and then proceed to slowly lower yourself taking about 10 seconds to perform the negative. Your effort should gradually increase with each rep and your speed should get faster until you are pulling up, but gravity is pulling you down against your best effort. When you can no longer go slower than about 4 seconds coming down, that is considered sufficient fatigue. I've also used this technique with much success on push ups for those that cannot do one

Resistance Training for Ice Hockey

or very many. Eventually, negative strength builds so much that positive push up repetitions become possible.

Negative Accentuated

This technique must be performed on a machine with fused movement arms. Many machines have movement arms that are independent like Hammer Strength. The performance of this technique is to lift bilaterally (with 2 limbs) and lower with only one. It is a great way to perform some negative only on your own without a partner. The movement arms must be fused so you are doubling the resistance lifted with 2 limbs and placing it on the only limb performing the negative. Alternate limbs descending on the negatives. It is a great technique and variable for biceps and triceps machines, but can be applied to any machine with a fused movement arm.

Partial range of motion reps

Over the years, it seems two schools of thought have emerged. Earlier fitness experts suggested moving in a full range of motion from full stretch to full contraction. More recently, the idea has emerged that you may be able to overload your neuromuscular system to a greater degree by using heavier loads and a shorter range of motion in your strongest portion of the range. Because we do not yet know which is better, resistance training involves the use of both of these techniques. And it is an opportunity to insert more variety anyway or work around injuries. Generally, a full range of motion is used on any one given exercise.

However, especially from a post-rehab point of view, a full range may not be desirable and possibly irritating to an otherwise already injured person. The positions of full stretch and full contraction are largely myths. Many muscles have multiple "heads" which requires the adjacent limbs to be in different positions to fully contract the different heads. We also believe that a majority of muscle fibers can be recruited in any position provided effort is high enough although this remains to be proven scientifically. We are not concerned with just inroading, fatiguing muscles, or loading them heavily. We are concerned with **ALL** of those aspects and the improvements from quality exercise seem to be a mixture of them all to differing degrees. The science is still in its infancy regarding these factors and their interconnected roles they play. Thus, all of these techniques have their place in a long term program.

Stage Reps

Partial range of motion reps can be a great variable to manipulate. Ellington Darden has referred to this as stage reps. You can divide the movement into halves or even into three different training zones. It makes sense to train to fatigue first your "weakest" zone. For example, perform 8-12 reps in the top half of the bicep curl to fatigue, then immediately perform 8-12 in the lower half to fatigue. Sometimes, you may reach fatigue 2 or 3 times within the same "set" of stage reps. The technique can be applied to machines and is particularly effective in working around sticking points with barbell exercises. Simply perform the stages and document your or your efforts on the progress chart. It is an interesting and different challenge.

Static Hold Training

Progressing with that line of thinking that a shorter range of motion could lead to better loading of the muscular structures, a non-moving static hold might be even better. Static hold training is different from regular isometric or static training. During that type of training, you are exerting effort against an immovable object. With static hold training, you are lifting your normal training weight or slightly more and holding it in a position that is advantageous leverage wise. I find with the pushing exercises that about two thirds of the way through the positive is a good position to hold and for pulling exercises, half way is good. For example, a chest press would place you with arms straight, but not locked. Slightly bent. About one third of the way back down the negative is where you'll hold. For a lat pulldown, you'll hold the bar with elbows bent about 90 degrees or bar about eye level. Which is half way back down the negative.

The reasons I like this method and especially for those training on their own are that it doesn't require as much focus on form because there is no form. All you have to concentrate on is staying positioned or aligned properly. In addition, it forces you to apply a more consistent and continuous contraction. The very fact that you are moving gives opportunity to unload and make the exercise less effective. You will also be bringing your muscles to fatigue on the negative as opposed to the positive which should make the fatigue a little more thorough. Indeed, one of the drawbacks to negative only training is that you have to unload to get back to the top position in order to lower again. Static hold training is a way around that problem. It also helps drive the point home that you are not just trying to move something and are trying to load the muscles against overloading resistance. I find this is the hardest concept to get across to trainees. Trying to move something while tired even though I am trying to get the trainee to a point where they can't move it, encourages bad form. This actually prevents the trainee's own progress because if they don't understand this, it ends up sloppy and I don't progress them because of poor control and form. I have been using this static hold technique with great success for my clients. I believe it is as good as or better than conventional means I described above even though, from what I can tell, there is relatively little research dedicated to the subject.

High repetition sets

Sometimes for an added challenge and a different level of intensity, we perform high repetition sets using ranges in the 15, 20, or even 30 rep area. A 20 rep barbell squat is one of the most challenging things anyone can do in a brief amount of time. Of course, this is along the muscular endurance side of the spectrum, but might also help to develop a little more fatigue in those that might not have inroaded so deeply with fewer reps or those that have a high percentage of slow twitch fibers.

Non-consecutive reps

Most of the time, we are striving for a set of consecutive repetitions. By consecutive, I mean, maintaining continuous muscular tension the whole time without respite at any point until muscular fatigue occurs. I have purposely avoided continuous tension with some surprising results too. It usually works well for those with poor motor control anyway, or low tolerance. I have used several forms of this. One is to perform a whole rep and set the weight down just long enough to take a breath and go again. Fatigue still occurs in a reasonable amount of time, but may help with some of the burning sensation. Physiologically, it might actually help to stave off some of the fatigue causing reactions and squeeze out another one or two productive reps. It's particularly effective on something like the leg extension or other exercises where it is not difficult to get started out of the bottom position from a dead stop.

Stop and go (Rest Pause)

This technique can be accomplished by performing a normal set of consecutive repetitions to fatigue followed by a 10 second rest and resuming a few more reps to fatigue. Continue two or three times. It has also been referred to as rest-pause. I don't think that's an accurate term. This technique may allow for the clearing of metabolic waste and by products in the 10 second rest and a few more follow up productive repetitions. In this case, we are deliberately letting go of muscular tension for very brief recovery purposes.

There is a second way to perform this. Instead of more consecutive reps after the first set to fatigue, if you get the resistance right and the effort is sufficient, the rest should be just long enough to allow 1 more near maximal rep at a time. For example, the leg press in a normal set to fatigue followed by a 10 second rest. Then perform 1 more near maximal rep followed by a 10 second rest. And repeat for as many follow up reps as you like or can.

Timed static contractions (TSC)

Although I don't believe this technique to be as effective, it still has its place and definitely is useful for the injured trainee. It is representative of original isometric training. This is different from a static hold whereby you are holding a specific amount of resistance. During TSC, you are just exerting against an immovable object. I like to use a method of graduated effort and intensity. I break the time frame up into 30 second blocks for a total of a minute and a half. The first 30 seconds is moderate effort, the second is about 90%, and the third is 100% all out effort. By the end of this, the inroading effect should be pretty high, but maybe not as effective as other techniques. We can thank Charles Atlas for popularizing this technique, but it has probably been around for centuries.

1 ¼ reps

This advanced technique is great for use on single joint exercises in general, but specifically for the arms and legs. It is simple really, you'll perform one whole positive, lower the bar ¼ of the way down, then squeeze back into the positive and contracted position then proceed down on a full negative. It's like doing a double squeeze technique. You'll probably need to lower the resistance a slight amount at first as you'll fatigue pretty quickly with this technique. Try it on leg curl, leg extension, bicep curl, and tricep extension.

Continuous tension contralateral reps

I got this technique from watching a demo video by Fred Fornicola of Premeire Personal Training. I don't know why I didn't think of it before. It's not simply alternating limbs like in doing DB arm curls in an alternating fashion. Again, to maintain continuous muscular tension, you can use this technique. Let's use the DB bicep curl as an example. You'll start with both DB's curled up. Do one whole negative and one whole positive back up to the start on one side. Holding that DB and that bicep in the contracted position under tension commence the negative and positive on the contralateral (opposite) side. Alternate and repeat. As with the technique above, you'll probably need to lower resistance a slight amount at first as you may experience more muscular tension and a faster rate of fatigue. A faster rate of fatigue = more intensity even with less resistance.

Akinetic training

Although this term could be used synonymously and in conjunction with infimetrics, I'll use it here in regards to the kinds of equipment most of us will have access to. This can be performed on some select Med-X equipment and older Nautilus equipment. More commonly, I've also used it with success on some types of pulley/cable equipment. Nautilus and Life Fitness, and I assume others; have a few equipment designs that involve "double pulleys". A lat pulldown or seated cable row apparatus where there are two pulleys instead of just one. However, the cable is connected from handle to handle via one cable at the weight stack. This is a must, the cable must be connected, not two separate cables to two separate weight stacks. This will allow you to lift the weight up to a pre-determined position. The object is to simultaneously extend one arm and flex the other while maintaining the weight stack at that pre-determined position without moving. Hence, the term "akinetic" meaning no movement. No movement of the selected resistance on the weight stack. Some machines have a pin hole or a block mechanism in place to press the weight stack up against, but it isn't necessary. It's similar to static contraction in a way, but this is external. The weight does not move, but the musculature will lengthen and shorten. In addition, it requires a little more motor control offers a different challenge.

Modified Squeeze Technique

One technique I like to employ especially for some beginners and sometimes on an area like the lower back is extending the time a client spends in the squeeze position on a single joint exercise. Although the lower back is not a single joint, per se, but the machinery we use operates like one. Instead of a one second pause and squeeze in the contracted position, you would have the client perform it for a longer amount of time say, three or five seconds. This can help the client in identifying the actual muscular structures that are supposed to be contracting and learning how to contract them better going forward in their training. It can help you learn the difference between simply pausing passively and actively squeezing in the contracted position. It can potentially add a little more effectiveness to the set. And in the case of the lower back, spending an extended time in that position, it can help make the trainee's back feel better by decompressing the discs. This can be critical for hockey players. Be sure to adjust resistance levels if necessary as this will cause fatigue quite a bit quicker than the usual squeeze technique.

Manual Resistance Reps

You can do virtually any equipment exercise, with some exceptions, in a manual fashion. There are some rules to follow. Be sure each partner understands. It is the trainee's responsibility to maintain control and change directions before reaching a point of over stretching as in neck exercises. Also, the trainee should not off/on their effort or suddenly give out on any exercise as the partner will still steadily be applying force. The partner must start slow gradually increasing force application with each rep until there is enough that the trainee will fatigue in the prescribed rep range. You may want to progressively work up to full range especially in the stretched position. For example, only go half way down on the first rep, slightly farther on the next, and then finally, a full but comfortable stretch on the 3rd or 4th rep. Be absolutely certain the client knows not to relax in the stretched position, but to maintain tension and perform a smooth and fluid change of direction into the next positive. Repeatedly mention this. It will be very tempting for them to let off suddenly while you are applying a fair amount of force. Remember also, that you need to vary the resistance. You should apply more force where they are stronger and slightly let off to allow them to complete the positive where they are weaker mechanically. To add an extra layer of difficulty, once you have developed a good bit of fatigue in the trainee, the partner can gradually decrease force application for an additional few reps. I've done this with the manual tricep extension until someone cannot even lift the weight of their forearm up and I'm barely touching their hand to apply resistance.

Make no mistake about this; manual training is a skill that is acquired with lots and lots of practice. Each trainee is a new experience and each one you will have to instruct and work with differently. Remember that wherever you are applying force to a person's body, you probably have a massive leverage advantage over them. You may not realize it, but just a slight push from you can place a HUGE amount of force on their tissues. This can especially be true in the neck. Sometimes, it may be just appropriate to start with the weight of the client's own limb or maybe just the weight of your hands. **Be extra extra careful. I cannot emphasize this enough.** There have been many instances of Yoga instructors pushing on clients in stretched positions and snapping their tendons off their bones. Not just Yoga, but anyone who doesn't fully appreciate the forces that you can impart from your hands through a person's limbs and onto their soft tissues. It may not be for everyone and it may be the only thing some can tolerate as a substitute for other movements. Use your judgment on each person and act prudently.

Infimetric

Infimetrics can be hard to visualize simply by the term. It is done with one side of the body working against the other side. It can also be done in a similar fashion to akinetic training using a pulley and 2 handles that are connected by the same cable or belt system. This can be similar to akinetic or the same in some instances. However, in this instance, we are referring to NOT using weight on a weight stack. You're simply resisting against your contralateral (opposite) side. Take a bicep curl for example, your right arm curls up while your left arm is forced down. The arm moving down is getting negative resistance while the other arm is simultaneously getting positive resistance. And because of the nature of your body, you'll always be able to resist more on the negative. Over time, you'll get stronger and be able to exert more force although it may not be that quantifiable. You can apply literally any amount of resistance and you can use any amount of speed of movement. It won't be explosive because one side is always resisting the other. This can be an infinite form of resistance and variety. There could be unlimited potential here.

Isometronic

Isometronic was developed by Peary Rader, the Iron Man magazine founder. It is a series of isometric or static contractions performed in short range movements. Here, a power rack can come into good use again. There are varieties of ways to perform it, but the easiest way is to do something like a bicep curl. Set the pins so that you curl the bar up and touch to the pins, but you cannot go beyond them. Try to break right through the pins with a maximal static contraction for 5-10 seconds. Perform a given rep range (8-12) in that position if you wish, but you don't have to. Then you can move the pins up to the next hole and progress through the range of motion using the same format. An alternative way is to load the bar with enough resistance that you can just curl it up to touch the pin and hold for 5-10 seconds. Then progress through the range.

Hyper

Hyper is another old Nautilus style of training technique. This is a very intense and maximal effort on both the positive and negative phases of each movement. It is very hard for a trainee to concentrate when performing this type of work and, in fact, some people may not be able to maintain the tension to perform it at all. You can use equipment with an appropriate load to be at or near maximal on the positive and you can provide more resistance manually on the negative as repetitions go on to elicit a maximal effort in both directions from the trainee. I prefer to use equipment, but only provide manual resistance to the bar so I can "feel" what the client is doing. The movement will be slow by default as it is a maximal effort both directions and they will quickly tire. Some repetitions may be as slow as 10 seconds on the positive and the negative. I use no more than 4 reps in this technique. You'll want to coach the trainee to continue to breathe openly and freely while maintaining tension and exerting maximally in

Resistance Training for Ice Hockey

both directions. Simple, but VERY intense. At the end of the exercise, the trainee will hardly be able to lift their arms or legs momentarily. You should find a position to get good leverage on the bar so you can overpower the trainee's effort. Your only limitation here, is your own strength.

Multiple planes of motion and/or hand grips

Not to go all the way into angle training philosophy, but there might be some benefit to using different planes or grip positions. Again, I have yet to see this definitively in scientific evidence, but it stands to reason that it can pay off. Here's how. We know that nothing is perfect, there are only trade offs. There will never be a perfect machine or exercise due to multiple muscle heads, joint shapes, and different hand grips required, etc. Like the supinated (underhand grip) lat pulldown may be a better grip for bicep strength, but it pulls the humerus bone (upper arm) OUT of the line of pull of the latissimus. The pronated grip keeps the humerus bone in more in the direct line of pull, but the bicep is in its weakest position. You see? It's only a trade off and you can't do both at the same time. Does it matter? Maybe not? Could it potentially matter in the long run? Sure. So here is a way to address the multiple functions. Actually there are more than one way, but this is one example. It is sort of along the same lines of reasoning as a breakdown technique which we do know from testing has been shown to be effective. Let's take the lat pulldown example again. The pronated grip is the weakest position, the neutral grip is the second strongest, and the supinated grip is the strongest position. So, instead of using one

39

grip and performing a breakdown in resistance used, I'll perform the "breakdown" using the different hand grips. In quick succession, I'll perform a pronated (overhand) grip (weakest position) lat pulldown with X weight. Keeping the same resistance, I'll switch to the neutral grip (second strongest), but I'm in a stronger position now, then perform the last in the supinated grip with the strongest position. In all instances, I was using a progressively stronger grip or hand position, but resistance staying the same even though I was fatiguing from each "set". So you get the effect of a breakdown and possible benefit of different angles or stimulation of muscular attachments. The same can be done on something like a chest press. Start with the decline, move to flat, then finally perform incline in the weakest position. You can use an infinite number of planes or hand grips that you wish. 3 should be sufficient for both.

Range Progression (More on Using the Power Rack)

One way to build very strong muscles and size is to make use of the power rack again except in this case, you are not using double or triple progression in terms of resistance, reps, or time. In this case, let's take the bench press for example, you select a resistance that is higher than you can perform now. Let's say 20-30% more than you can lift positively. Instead of doing full range dynamic reps trying to increase up to that, although that will work, you can start at the top and work down, so to speak. Set the bar with the given resistance at the top end of the movement. Set the pins to the shortest range possible. Perform a dynamic, but short range movement to positive fatigue. Over time and from workout to workout, you KEEP the same resistance and MOVE THE PINS DOWN one hole at a time. So your progression is in the form of range of motion, not the other variables. Over time, you should be able to lower down and press back up what you previously could not positively lift at all. This may be one of the quickest and most effective ways to gain strength quickly.

All of these advanced techniques are available to you to provide variety and methods to work around certain issues or stimulate new progress. You can use each one of them individually or even combine some of them for very intense work. For example, sometimes in a single "set" of an exercise, I'll try to fatigue the client's positive, static, and negative strength. Or go in that reverse order. This is an intense effort and very thorough level of fatigue. It can help with those that may not have the ability to muster the output on their own in one dynamic set to positive fatigue.

Beware of overtraining

All of these variables can be put to use during the lifespan of a hockey trainee's program. A word of caution though, overtraining is easier to do than people think. Use advanced techniques sparingly. I have used them for weeks on end, but be conscious and aware of your responses and progress. Some general overtraining symptoms are:

- Trouble going to sleep
- Trouble waking up

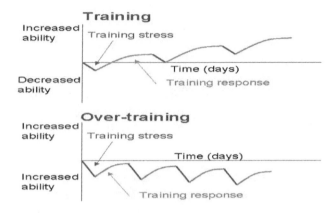

- Overuse atrophy
- Lack of performance
- Irritability
- Depression
- Elevated resting heart rate
- Persistent soreness
- Decreased appetite
- Injuries
- Decreased immunity

All of these symptoms can be vague and already common, especially in young athletes. It isn't unlike adolescents to be irritable and depressed. Keep a close eye on things and look for changes. Try to really be in tune with your own body or the bodies and attitudes of your athletes if you're a coach.

Everyone is different, pay attention to what your body is trying to tell you. Be conscious and aware. Once a person delves into overtraining, it takes time to get out. Think of it like digging a hole, the deeper you go, the longer it takes to climb out.

If you do find yourself overtrained, as many people

Resistance Training for Ice Hockey

are, your best bet is a week or so off.

RESISTANCE TRAINING FOR HOCKEY ROUTINES

At this point, take a look at the routines included in your folder. Each one is to be performed for 2 weeks and they will be numbered routines 1-4 so they are easy for you to follow.

If you have a question as to what an exercise looks like, refer to our exercise picture database below. Let's take the first routine and go over the details of each exercise. You'll want to complete each exercise and routine with the same level of detail as you progress forward in your training.

Leg Curl

I prefer to use the prone leg curl as the seated version presents some biomechanical problems, but it is an OK substitute especially if used with a static hold technique. You should enter between the movement arm and the body padding facing the body padding. To achieve axial alignment of the knee and the apparatus, the superior aspect of the patella (top of knee cap) should be just below the body padding. You can gradually walk your hands out and lie down prone on the padding. The movement arm padding should fall onto the achilles area, but not on the heel, itself or too far up the calf. Proper alignment is achieved if there is relatively little pad rolling up or down the leg during the excursion. You can look straight down at the pad or use a pad against the forehead to achieve neutral spinal alignment throughout the exercise.

Your hands should be hooked on the handles without excessive gripping to maintain body position. You should perform a 1 second squeeze technique at the top end of the range and repetition for a little added effectiveness. Perform smooth, slow, controlled repetitions at a 2/4 cadence in the chosen rep range (8-12) to volitional fatigue or until movement is almost not possible. You can then set the movement arm down, walk your hands up the padding to stand up, and exit through the side of the machine in the same way you entered. Questions to ask yourself while going through the process to ensure good form are: Are you relaxing uninvolved structures? Are you breathing properly? Are your reps slow and controlled? Are you using both limbs equally or shifting? Are you concentrating or trying to take your mind off the activity? Did you inroad your strength to a sufficient degree?

Leg Press

You should enter by sitting on the seat pad and lifting the legs up onto the foot plate. You can then pull the release lever and gradually slide them forward (on many machines) until an approximate 90 degree angle is achieved in the knee joint. You should begin the positive over the course of two seconds without a sudden jerk at the weight continuing into the upper turnaround WITHOUT a pause. If you lock the knee, you will relax. The object is to maintain muscular tension throughout. After a smooth upper turnaround, commence the negative over a 4 second duration bringing the resistance down to lightly bottom out the weight stack, but again without relaxing the musculature.

Breathe openly and continuously. Continue well controlled reps to positive muscular fatigue in the 8-20 rep range with a 2/4 cadence. Exit the machine carefully and be sure to be careful when you try to walk as you nearly exhausted all of your leg strength. You don't want to hit the ground as you begin to walk away. It could happen.

Reverse Grip Lat Pulldown

Begin by entering the machine by grabbing hold of the bar in an underhand fashion about shoulder width. Sit down while pulling the bar part way down. Lock the thighs under the thigh restraint pads. You are ready to begin the exercise. Perform by lifting the weight in the positive over the course of two seconds. Note: In this case, the positive is the weight going up, but the arms are moving down. The positive is when the weight is going up on every exercise, not what the body is doing. You should pull the resistance toward the top of the sternum or bottom of the neck and pause and squeeze after a couple of submaximal reps. This is a compound exercise, but it is OK to squeeze as the muscles are in the contracted position at the top end of the movement (when bar is closest to the chest). Proceed through the negative over 4 seconds under control and while depressing the shoulders and extending the elbows to maintain tension on the latissimus muscles. When the elbow is almost completely straight, have smoothly turn around and perform the next positive. The scapula should rotate upward and downward, but the shoulder girdle should not elevate (no shrugging). To exit the machine after positive fatigue, extend your elbows and slowly stand to set the weight down.

Chest Press

Set the seat height so that the bar comes across your sternum level. You should be able to grip the bar with a moderately wide grip and have your elbows directly behind the wrist to travel in a relatively linear fashion. The seat back should be set so that the bar does not over stretch you, but such that you can comfortably bottom out the weight stack each rep. Record the 2 seat settings. Perform slow controlled reps at a 2/4 cadence with no pause or stop at the top of the movement and without locking out the elbows to maintain pectoralis and tricep tension. The spine should be neutral or extended, the chest high, shoulders depressed, and the cervical spine neutral. Once positive fatigue is reached, set the weight stack down carefully and stand up to exit the exercise.

Compound Row

This is a cable apparatus, but the machine version can be used as well. Sit on the bench and lean forward to grab the neutral grip handle. You can use whatever grip you like here, but generally neutral grip is common. Supinated grip is best for bicep strength as in reverse grip for the lat pulldown. I prefer neutral grip after performance of lat pulldown already. You should have legs almost straight to allow the cable and handle to pass by. You should sit chest high with extended back and shoulders retracted and depressed. Do not lean forward to flex at the hip when performing the negative. Perform slow smooth controlled reps to fatigue with 2/4 cadence. You should lean forward to set the weight down under control and carefully stand up off the bench to exit.

Tricep Extension

The proper term for this is elbow extension, but there are many variations. I prefer the cable pressdown with the rope handle. This allows you to best keep your elbows at your sides and not turn it into a pressing movement and keep it rotary. You should stand so that the elbow does not move forward as the negative is performed. Again, the positive is when the weight is going up, not what the body is doing. At the top of the movement, perform a squeeze technique for the triceps. You should perform slow controlled reps in a 2/4 cadence to positive fatigue. Note: this exercise may not last many reps as there has already been a couple of tricep exercises. The chest press and even the two compound pulling exercises involve the long head of the triceps that crosses the shoulder joint and contributes to shoulder extension in the pulldown and row. When positive fatigue is reached set the weight down and walk away.

Bicep Curl

Sit in the machine at the appropriate height so that your elbows align with the axis of the machine. You should take an underhand grip on the handles with a neutral wrist. You will commence the positive over a 2 second time span and pausing and squeezing at the top of the movement after a couple of submaximal reps. Perform the negative over a 4 second duration without elevating the shoulder, thus, allowing the biceps tissues to stretch. Continue slow controlled reps to positive fatigue and have slowly set the weight down to exit the machine. Here too, there may not be a lot of reps as there have been a couple of bicep involved exercises already.

Lower Back Extension

You want to be careful with this exercise. It is not inherently dangerous, but it is a sensitive spot and has the potential to aggravate an existing condition . I'll describe the model to the right. Position the foot pedestal high enough that you can safely climb in and buckle the seat belt. When you gradually begin the positive, your hips should extend pressing up into the seat belt while maintaining a flat foot and slightly bent knee. You should exaggerate the extending motion pushing your chest up to the ceiling and upper back down toward the floor. Pause and squeeze in the contracted position after a couple submaximal reps then commence the negative taking 4 seconds to lower the weight. Lightly bottom out the resistance and start again. The back pad is aligned properly if it does not roll up and down your back during the excursion.

Abdominal Crunch

Position the seat height so that the machine axis is approximately belly button level. Try to slump slightly and flex just the lumbar spine versus trying to lean all the way forward and bend at the hip. Some of that may happen, but the rectus abdominus flexes the lumbar spine and that is the function you should strive for. The positive is performed in a slow smooth movement over 2 seconds with a pause and squeeze technique after a couple of submaximal reps. The negative is performed over 4 seconds. Barely touch the weight stack to bottom out and begin the next positive. Continue to positive fatigue. Carefully stand up and exit the machine.

Calf Raise

I prefer to use the bottom edge of the foot plate on the leg press machine or a specific calf raise machine for this exercise as opposed to the standing calf raise machine. The pads load the shoulders and compress the spine and if you are a middle aged person with some degree of spinal degeneration, it may irritate. Spinal compression is probably not good for the hockey athlete either. Stick to the other models that do not load through the shoulders and spine. Enter the machine by sitting on the seat and the ball of your foot should be right at the edge of the foot plate, but definitely on the plate, not hanging off. Perform a 2 second positive with a pause and squeeze technique in the contracted position after a couple submaximal reps. The first negative should be just a slight stretch, the second a little deeper, and the third you can go into full stretch. The Achilles tendon is the biggest tendon in the body and you want to protect it by gradually increasing the range of the stretch as well as making absolutely certain that you do not explode out of the stretch or do anything sudden or jerky. Perform 8-12 slow controlled reps to positive fatigue. Put your feet down and swing one leg over the bar, both feet on the ground, stand and walk away from the machine. Be careful when you walk as severely weakened calf muscles will alter your gait.

Rotary Torso

There are likely two versions of this exercise. You'll want to have a seat on the machines seat. There are two "sides" to this exercise. Meaning that you'll perform two sets almost. What you don't want to do is go all the way from one side to the other bouncing the weight stack off the bottom in the middle of the rep.

Sit in the seat, if it is the version where your upper body rotates, place your arms inside of the padding. Lift the lever and rotate your chest, shoulders, and head to one side as far as you comfortably can and lock it in place.

If it is the version where the lower body moves like the Life Fitness version, do the same except keep your chest and shoulders square to the immovable pad in front of your and turn your lower body out to one side and lock it in.

Trying to keep your head and neck in alignment, slowly tighten your mid-section muscles to gradually turn back the opposite direction. Don't look where you are going. Look straight ahead where your chest is pointing. Sit tall and extended. Squeeze your mid-section muscles in the contracted position against the resistance and slowly lower back down over 4 sections. Very lightly touch the weight stack down, but don't unload or go farther than where it bottoms out and

Resistance Training for Ice Hockey

smoothly transition to the next positive.

Continue to perform as many good reps as possible in an 8-12 rep range to positive muscular fatigue. Then lift the lever and rotate an equal distance to the other side and perform the same technique for the opposite side.

It won't matter terribly which option you choose or have access to. I tend to prefer the version where the upper body rotates rather than the lower body, but both will address the mid-section structures appropriately.

With this routine, you've successfully addressed all of the major muscle groups and specifically focused on mid-section musculature in four directions and increased trunk rotation strength.

We've designed a routine that can improve your muscular strength, enhance your flexibility, and address cardiovascular and metabolic conditioning if you move quickly between exercises.

We start with the larger muscle groups and work down to smaller ones in a push/pull fashion so you can quickly get to the next exercise without having to stop and rest the opposing muscle group you just worked.

This routine should be highly applicable to someone engaging in the sport of hockey and offer not only performance improvement (strength, not skill), but also some injury prevention particularly of the lower back and knees.

Refer to your routines below and continue them on the schedule laid out above using these same principles regardless of the exercise listed.

Hockey Routine 2

Leg Press or Squat
Leg Curl
Leg Ext.
Calf Raise
Hip ABduction/ADduction
Hip Flexion
Overhand Grip Lat Pulldown
Overhead (Shoulder) Machine Press
Dumbbell Lateral Raise
Barbell Bicep Curl
Abdominal Crunch
Lower Back Extension
BB Wrist Extension
BB Wrist Flexion

Hockey Routine 3

BB Deadlift
Calf Raise
Hip ABduction/ADduction
Leg Extension
BB Bench Press (Use Power Rack)
Chest Fly Machine
Cable Tricep Pressdown
DB 1 Arm Row
Machine or Cable Super Pullover
DB Bicep Curl
Rotary Torso
Lower Back Extension
Manual Neck Extension and Flexion

Hockey Routine 4

BB Squat
Machine Abdominal Crunch
Lower Back Extension
Rotary Torso
Cable Row
BB Bench Press or Chest Press
Negative Only Chins
DB Overhead Press
BB Wrist Extension
BB Wrist Flexion
Hanging Hip Flexion
BB Straight Leg Deadlift
BB Shrug
Manual Neck Flexion

Seasonal Training

These are off season, full body routines that can be performed to muscular fatigue and beyond as often as 3 days per week. This can be done spring through summer.

In season training schedules will likely need to be reduced and slightly less intense. Training one or two days per week is going to be appropriate. The goal here is to maintain what has been built up. It is reasonable to expect yourself or your team to lose several pounds of both fat and lean tissue over the course of a season due to the stress involved.

For a short time leading up to a training camp or start of a season, you can train as often as six days a week at a high intensity as long as you allow for local recovery. An alternating schedule of upper body and lower body every day of the week except one complete rest day can allow for a quick increase in fitness immediately preceding the season. I would suggest keeping this time period short around the two week time length so as not to overreach or overtrain immediately prior to the season.

Think of your training schedule in 3 phases:

Phase 1 Off Season
Phase 2 Pre-season
Phase 3 In Season

Recognize the cumulative stresses and subsequent rest periods you'll be afforded with this schedule and manage your training schedule and intensities appropriately. You can't do it all, all of the time. Off season is about building and progress. Pre-season is about reaching a peak. In season is about maintaining and focusing on maximized performance.

Immediately post-season is a time of reflection and rest and recuperation from a long and stressful season. Take the time to allow that recovery. The more you've cumulatively stressed your body or your athletes, the more time it will take to fully recover. Don't make the mistake of jumping right into intense off season work. All the recovery, then gradually work up to a building off season phase again.

Resistance Training for Ice Hockey

COACHING AND ON ICE PRACTICE SPECIFICS

Knowing what I know now, I would have structured my own training and practice pretty differently from when I was growing up. I always had good coaches and, for the most part, they were doing it on a volunteer basis. I certainly cannot fault them. But, I'd do things differently now that I've learned what I've learned. I'd keep it simple, but extremely effective.

I think there are a couple of mistakes most coaches make:

1. **They get sucked into extravagant, complicated, and irrelevant drills from coaching magazines and seminars.**
2. **They use conditioning as punishment and scrimmage as a reward.**

These 2 mistakes can completely alleviate the fun the players have from the experience. We all know, players play best when they are healthy and having a good time. We need to cultivate that.
I would structure a practice the same at almost any level. Simplicity is key. A 700 page playbook may only serve to confuse and frustrate your players.
First of all, I'd avoid the first mistake. The entire point of practice is to get better at the actual game. Rarely does a practice resemble an actual game except when? In a scrimmage. That's right. All players love to scrimmage because they love the game. We'll get back to this in a second.

If you remember in our first chapter, we talked

about specificity. It's also a mistake to engage in high intensity conditioning skating drills in the beginning of practice. Why? Because when you get to the fine skill practice, every player will be fatigued and probably shaky. You want to practice motor skills in the best possible state, not the worst. Yes, it's true in a game, fatigue will set in and you will still have to perform. But, practicing in a perpetually fatigued state every practice will serve to lessen a player's skill. When I was younger playing junior hockey we had a whole season of practice organized like this and I believe we actually ended up worse at the end of the season skill wise.

Conversely, when we were about 16 years old, a teammate said to me in warm ups one day that he thought when we scrimmaged, it was our best practice. We didn't realize it at the time, but he was exactly right and we had no idea the truth in his statement.

So much of coaching is about tradition. Little science or free thinking is involved in the process. So let's inject some logic into it. Once again, if the point of practice is to get better at the actual game, wouldn't you want to make it look like it?

Resistance Training for Ice Hockey

PRACTICE STRATEGY

How to organize a 90 minute practice

30 minutes

- Light warm up (no stretching)
- Skill practice
  - Skating (power and technique)
  - Shooting (power and accuracy)
  - Passing (accuracy)
  - Checking (body, fore, back)
- Team playbook
  - Set plays
    - Breakout
    - Neutral zone play
    - Even/odd man rushes
    - Corner/slot play
    - Offensive strategy
    - Defensive strategy
  - Special teams
    - 5 on 4
    - 5 on 3
    - 4 on 4
    - 4 on 3
    - Penalty kill of above scenarios
    - All 3 zones of play

60 Minutes

- Scrimmage
  - First line mostly plays fourth line
  - Full contact

- Keep score
- Same sense of intensity and urgency as a real game
- Penalties can be called
- Uneven strength can be played

5 Minutes

- Optional stretching and cool down

DON'T get sucked into a bunch of drills that don't look like a hockey game or condition players for one. The bulleted items above under skill practice should resemble game situations except that they are broken out from a real game. It should look like a skill you can repeat over and over again so each player learns what to do in each situation when he actually encounters it in a game. Long complicated drills that don't all go the same direction and use things like multiple pucks, multiple lines of players, and passes, are ridiculous and confusing. Practice of odd man rushes should look like odd man rushes in a game with real back checkers coming on the way for a real sense of speed and urgency. What you are doing is only pulling one piece of the game out that is a specific skill or set play and rehearsing it over and over again until you get your style down and the players do it almost by habit. It's about specificity. Make your drills specific to the skill or play and just like the players would encounter in a game. If it isn't exactly like a real game, it isn't practice for a real game. This is the essence of perfect practice.

Yes, it's a little bit of a risk to play full contact in each practice, but in order to get better at the actual game, we need to create the same sense of intensity and urgency. Otherwise, you are practicing in a subpar manner for when you encounter a real motivated opponent. In football, we have no coaching qualms about playing full contact in practice, we shouldn't in hockey either. It's a full contact game, practice it as such within reason and with a concern for player safety.

Why the first line playing the fourth line? Because, the best and fastest way to increase a player's skill is to forcefully drop him into an environment to where he is surrounded by those better than him. He MUST improve quickly in order to even survive out there. When I was growing up, I always played "up", both in terms of skill level and age. I rapidly improved all of my skills especially skating and speed. It will ready players for a much faster pace of game they will encounter from more talented or experienced opponents.

Your players will be competitive, a little intrasquad competition is a good thing. But, they will also be brothers and sisters. It's also no secret that the more talented players tend to rely on that. Fourth line players may be less skilled overall, but many times have greater work ethics. Playing these two lines against each other will result in an improvement in the skill or effort level the other one lacks. The first liners don't want to be out played by the fourth liners. They will try hard not to be outplayed. They also don't want to lose their spot on the first line. The fourth liners are hard working, competitive players and want to move up to higher lines. Use their natural positions on specific lines and their attitudes against each other to better each other. As coach, shuffle your lines and player positions accordingly to performance in practice, everyone being given ample chances. Each practice can serve as a new try out for upcoming games. Some players will have slumps, some will be on fire. Manage their playing abilities according to recent performance and attitude. Chances are here, you'll have a team with great depth and any line could play against any other line and be relatively evenly matched. If every line you have is your first line, you'll be a winning coach.

When I was younger, we were all set to have a really good midget AA team. We were excited and confident. Many of those players trying out were Bantams playing up as well. It turned out that our Junior B team did not have enough players and our league wanted us to forego a Midget team and field a Junior B team. So we did. It resulted in us being in high school with players as young as 15 playing Junior hockey. That's not all that uncommon, but we were a whole team of them. We were the Southernmost team in the league. Every weekend, we travelled up North to play teams who were much older, faster, stronger, better in almost every way. We did well. We held our own. We weren't champions, but one thing was clear. We had to improve quite rapidly in order to overcome our disadvantages. Essentially, we were boys playing grown men. We even joked about the players from other teams showing up to our games with their wives and kids.

You might think "What about the first line? Isn't this coaching them down?" It could be. But, chances are, in many places, ice time is at a premium.

What happens here is that two teams may share an ice time. Often these will be teams from the same club. If you're a coach, work with the other coaching staff and let them know about how you organize practice. See if you can take advantage of the other team's skilled players to pit them against your first line. This comes in very handy if the other team at practice is an age group older. If you can have your Bantam team scrimmage the club's Midget team, or your B team scrimmage the A team, you'll rapidly increase the skill of your own players.

The point is to pit your best players against the less skilled and FORCE improvement. Either intrasquad scrimmages on your own team or intersquad within your club's various levels and ages can be used.

You don't want players to be in the dark. You want to give them some consistency and know what to expect. Confused players don't make champions. You want them to have some regularity and probably be able to know how to run a practice even without you there. They'll know what to do right when they get on the ice. And you'll have built in motivation for effort, skill, and performance due to the competitive nature of the scrimmage. The players will have a great time because they are playing the game they love. They will develop specific conditioning to a high intensity, full speed, 60 minute game in which you are practicing for. They won't waste time on non-specific, drawn out, unlikely drill scenarios or any number of other things that won't contribute directly to their improvement as players.

You now have a system which has built in conditioning and motivation that can be done in a repeatable process maybe even without you, the coach, present. Ultimately, you're the coach. You can take this general outline and re-organize it to your heart's content to suit your needs. Remember, to keep it specific and keep it simple and both you and your players will do well and have fun.

So there you have it. We've accomplished a lot here. We've decided on what not to do. We've established some basic principles to follow. We've provided a variety of modes and equipment on which to train. We've established some advanced training for long term progress and variety. And we've established some specific routines to start with to address the parts of the body specific to the sport of hockey. Be sure to review the pictures and video provided below and remember to track your results on your progress chart. Most of all, give it a good effort and up your game while staying fit and injury free.

Thank you and good luck out there on the ice!

Resistance Training for Ice Hockey

EXERCISE PICTURE DEMONSTRATIONS

LOWER BODY EXERCISES

Resistance Training for Ice Hockey

Trap Bar Dead Lift Start

Trap Bar Dead Lift Finish

Weighted Calf Raise Start

Weighted Calf Raise Finish

Resistance Training for Ice Hockey

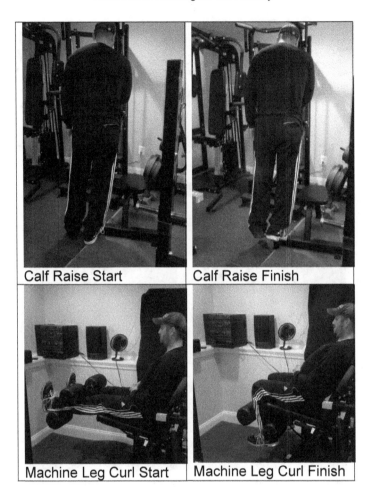

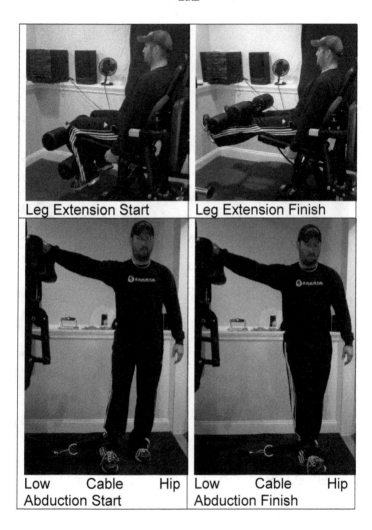

Resistance Training for Ice Hockey

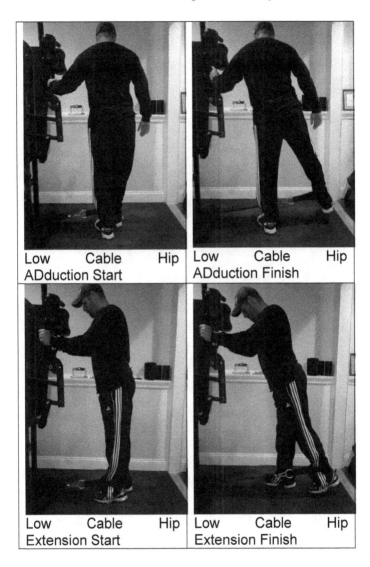

CHEST SHOULDER AND TRICEP EXERCISES

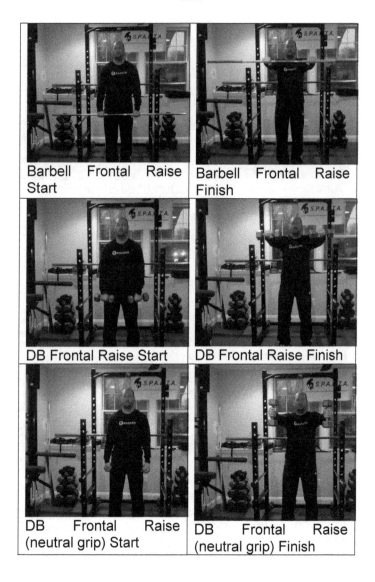

 DB Rear Deltoid Start	 DB Rear Deltoid Finish
 DB Rear Deltoid (overhand grip) Start	 DB Rear Deltoid (overhand grip) Finish
 Barbell Overhead Press (shoulder press/military press) Start	 Barbell Overhead Press (shoulder press/military press) Finish

DB Overhead Press Start

DB Overhead Press Finish

DB Overhead Press (neutral grip) Start

DB Overhead Press (neutral grip) Finish

Machine Overhead Press Start

Machine Overhead Press Finish

Incline DB Chest Fly Start

Incline DB Chest Fly Finish

Incline Barbell Chest Press Start

Incline Barbell Chest Press Finish

Flat DB Chest Fly Start

Flat DB Chest Fly Finish

Resistance Training for Ice Hockey

Resistance Training for Ice Hockey

Behind the Head DB Tricep Extension Start

Behind the Head Tricep Extension Finish

Behind the Head Barbell Tricep Extension Start	Behind the Head Barbell Tricep Extension Finish

Behind the Head Low Cable Tricep Extension Start	Behind the Head Low Cable Tricep Extension Finish

UPPER BACK, REAR SHOULDER, BICEP EXERCISES

Resistance Training for Ice Hockey

| Straight Arm Pulldown Start | Straight Arm Pulldown Finish |
| Overhand Grip Lat Pulldown Start | Overhand Grip Lat Pulldown Finish |

Resistance Training for Ice Hockey

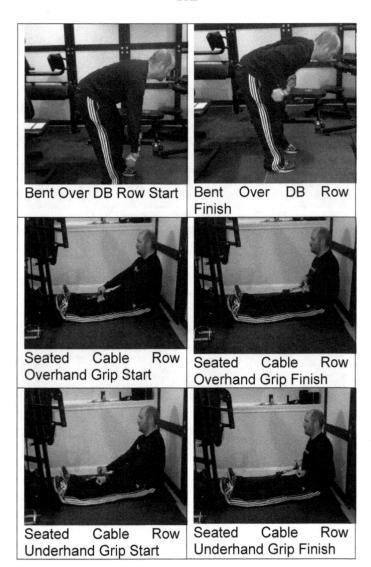

Resistance Training for Ice Hockey

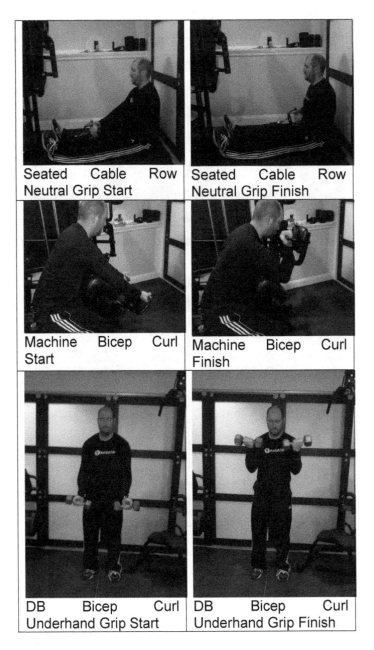

 DB Bicep Curl Neutral Grip Start	 DB Bicep Curl Neutral Grip Finish
 DB Bicep Curl Overhand Grip Start	 DB Bicep Curl Overhand Grip Finish

Resistance Training for Ice Hockey

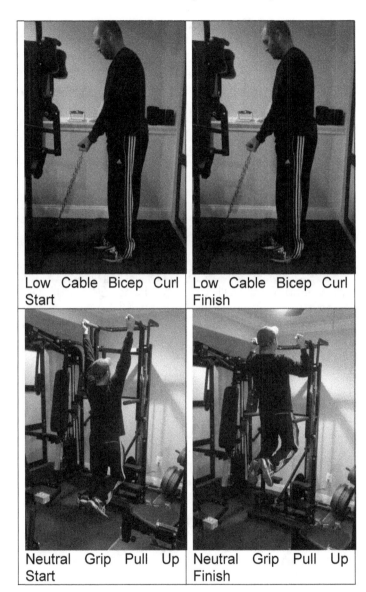

Low Cable Bicep Curl Start | Low Cable Bicep Curl Finish

Neutral Grip Pull Up Start | Neutral Grip Pull Up Finish

 Overhand Grip Pull Up Start	 Overhand Grip Pull Up Finish
 Underhand Grip Chin Up Start	 Underhand Grip Chin Up Finish

ABDOMINAL, LOWER BACK, AND NECK EXERCISES

Manual Neck Extension Start

Manual Neck Extension Finish

Manual Neck Flexion Start

Manual Neck Flexion Finish

Resistance Training for Ice Hockey

DB Weighted Crunch Start	DB Weighted Crunch Finish
Abdominal Cable Crunch	Abdominal Cable Crunch
Double Crunch Start	Double Crunch Finish

Low Cable Oblique Side Bend Start

Low Cable Oblique Side Bend Finish

DB Oblique Side Bend Start

DB Oblique Side Bend Finish

Low Cable Straight Leg Dead Lift Start

Low Cable Straight Leg Dead Lift Finish

Barbell Straight Leg Dead Lift Start

Barbell Straight Leg Dead Lift Finish

DB Straight Leg Dead Lift Start | DB Straight Leg Dead Lift Finish

Hip Flexion Start | Hip Flexion Finish

One Leg Hip Flexion Start

One Leg Hip Flexion Finish

Parallel Bar Hip Flexion Start

Parallel Bar Hip Flexion Finish

Hanging Hip Flexion Start | Hanging Hip Flexion Finish

RESISTANCE TRAINING FOR HOCKEY PROGRESS CHART

S.P.A.R.T.A.
Sports Performance And Resistance Training Association

Name:

Phone:

Goals:

Exercises/Settings:	Date: Weight:									

Notes:

Measure Date: _____ Arm: _____ Chest: _____ Waist: _____ Hip: _____ Thigh: _____ Body Fat: ___ , ___ , ___ = _____ = _____ %

Use the chart above to document your or your team's training performance. You can simply document dates, exercises, sets, and reps. Or take more detailed notes in the spaces provided for other performance measures or anthropometrics.

Feel free to make a chart like this of your own. But, if you'd like a copy you can use, click here to download and print as many as you need.
Progress Chart - http://bit.ly/2bW0kdR

ABOUT THE AUTHOR

Chris Lutz is the owner and founder of **S.P.A.R.T.A. – Sports Performance And Resistance Training Association.** Teaching, reading and writing about proper exercise methodology are his biggest passions.

Chris is nationally certified as a Certified Personal Trainer. He has also developed a specialized training certification. He attended George Mason University and obtained a Bachelor of Science in Exercise Science from the Health, Fitness, and Recreation Resources Dept. in Fairfax, VA 2000 – 2004.

Chris' combination of B.S. degree, high intensity training CPT certification, and over 5 years of experience managing a training facility, and owning a business earned him his Master Trainer status.

Chris is also the author of other books for the fitness industry and the general public.

www.ingramcontent.com/pod-product-compliance
Lightning Source LLC
LaVergne TN
LVHW012207050325
805250LV00032B/713